D1530033

JUL 2 6 2017

Little Inventions

THE FORK

RAPHAËL FEJTÖ

FIREFLY BOOKS

A long time ago, in Greek and Roman times, a type of fork called the *harpago* was used in kitchens to pick up meat to check if it was well cooked.

But it did not leave the kitchen and no one would have thought of using it to eat their meal!

In the West, people only ate with their fingers! And that went on for centuries and centuries...

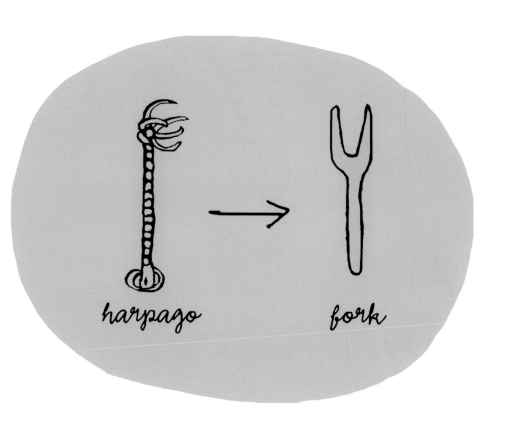

harpago

fork

Then, in the Byzantine Empire, the *harpago* went through a transformation and became a small two-pronged fork that was used for eating. In Europe, however, the *harpago* was still in use, and only used for cooking.

One day, the Byzantine princess, Theodora Doukas, married the *doge*, or prince, of Venice and was very surprised to learn that no one used forks in Italy.

So, she decided to have a blacksmith make her a gold fork.

The *doge* of Venice was very surprised by
the bizarre object he was supposed to eat
with. He agreed to use it because his wife
really insisted upon it.

The fork pleased the people who came
to see the princess and gradually, it
became very popular in Italy.

But this trend was only in Italy, and in France, most people continued to eat with their fingers.

Aristocrats at the court...

...like the peasants in the country.

One day, the king of France, Henry the 3rd, took a trip to Florence and discovered a fork at his host's table.

He learned that in Italy, it was used because it was very practical for eating spaghetti. So, Henry the 3rd decided to bring one back to France.

The king was very happy since, thanks to his fork, he didn't get stains on his big white collar, which was very fashionable at the time, called a *fraise*.

Proud of his new find, he showed it to his friends who didn't understand why their king loved spending his time with it.

Very excited, he went to eat
at his favorite restaurant in
Paris, The Silver Tower, so
everyone could see him with
his new object.

But people didn't understand why their king loved this fork. They all thought it was ridiculous.

His mother, Catherine de Médici, did not appreciate that her son ate with it either. But the king did not care at all, he was sure people would eventually understand that this object was awesome!

Years later, King Louis the 14th also thought it was a nice object, so he ordered his servants to always put a fork beside his plate.

But the king didn't use it, he preferred eating with his fingers. Forks were only used as a decoration on the table!

For many years, the fork was placed on the table but nobody knew exactly what to do with it.

Finally, it was decided that it should be used to pick one's teeth at the end of a meal.

Then people started using the fork to pierce their food... before putting it in their mouth with their fingers!

At the end of the 17th century, the fork was perfected and transitioned from two, to three, and then four prongs.

It was more practical to bring food directly to the mouth, so the people of the court finally used the fork to eat! And that is how the fork gradually became a huge success.

The fork is always placed to the left of the plate with the prongs against the table for the French, and the prongs facing up for the English. This is because, in the past, nobles and kings had their coat of arms engraved on the back of the fork's neck in France, and on the front in England.

French style

English style

Today, many types of forks exist, depending on what you're eating: forks for meat, fish, cheese... and even dessert forks!

And you? What's your favorite

?

There you go, now you know everything about the invention of the fork!

But do you remember everything you've read?

Play the MEMORY Game to see what you remember!

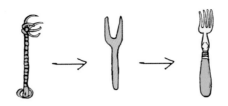

MEMORY GAME

1. What was the fork called in Greek and Roman times?

2. What was the first fork used for in Roman times?

3. How many prongs did the first fork have?

4. In which country did Henry the 3rd discover the fork?

5. What did Louis XIV do with his fork?

1. The *harpago*
2. To pick up meat to see if it was well cooked
3. Two
4. Italy
5. Nothing! It was only used as a decoration!

A FIREFLY BOOK

Published by Firefly Books Ltd. 2016

Source edition © 2015 La Forchette, ÉDITIONS PLAY BAC, 33 rue du Petit-Musc, 75004, Paris, France, 2015

This translated edition copyright © 2016 Firefly Books

First printing

Publisher Cataloging-in-Publication Data (U.S.)

Names: Fejtö, Raphaël, author | Greenspoon, Golda, translator. | Mersereau, Claudine, translator.
Title: Fork / Raphaël Fejtö.
Description: Richmond Hill, Ontario, Canada : Firefly Books, 2016. | Series: Little Inventions | Originally published by Éditions Play Bac, Paris, 2015 as Les p'tites inventions: La Fourchette | Summary: "This brief history on one of the small, overlooked inventions we use in our everyday lives, in a six-part series is geared toward children. With fun and quirky illustrations and dialog, it also comes with a memory quiz to ensure children retain what they learn" -- Provided by publisher.
Identifiers: ISBN 978-1-77085-745-2 (hardcover)
Subjects: LCSH: Forks – History -- Juvenile literature. | Kitchen utensils – History – Juvenile literature.
Classification: LCC TX656.F458 |DDC 683.82 – dc23

Library and Archives Canada Cataloguing in Publication

Fejtö, Raphaël
[Fourchette. English]
    Fork / Raphaël Fejtö.
(Little inventions)
Translation of: La fourchette.
ISBN 978-1-77085-745-2 (bound)
    1. Forks--History--Juvenile literature. I. Title.
II. Title: Fourchette. English.
TX656.F4613 2016   j642'.7   C2016-900077-X

Published in the United States by
Firefly Books (U.S.) Inc.
P.O. Box 1338, Ellicott Station
Buffalo, New York 14205

Published in Canada by
Firefly Books Ltd.
50 Staples Avenue, Unit 1
Richmond Hill, Ontario L4B 0A7

Printed in China

E642.7
Fej

playBac

les p'tites inventions